Lyrical Diagrams

Also by David Greenslade

Prose
Fishbone (Y Wasg Israddol, 1993)
Creosote ('Iwo Rivers Press, 1996)
Cambrian Country (Gwasg Carreg Gwalch, 2000)

Verse
Old Emulsion Customs (Y Wasg Israddol, 1998)
Each Broken Object (Two Rivers Press, 2000)
Weak Eros (Parthian, 2002)
Adventure Holiday (Parthian, 2007)
Zeus Amoeba (Two Rivers Press, 2009)
Homuncular Misfit (PS Avalon, 2011)

In Welsh
Yr Wyddor (Gomer Press, 1998)
March (Y Wasg Israddol, 1998)
Pebyll/Pavellons (Y Wasg Israddol, 1995)

Novel
Celtic Hot Tub (Gwasg Carreg Gwalch, 2003)

David Greenslade

Lyrical Diagrams

Images
by
Carolina Vasquez

Shearsman Books

First published in the United Kingdom in 2012 by
Shearsman Books
50 Westons Hill Drive
Emersons Green
Bristol
BS16 7DF

Shearsman Books Ltd Registered Office
30–31 St. James Place, Mangotsfield, Bristol BS16 9JB
(this address not for correspondence)

www.shearsman.com

ISBN 978-1-84861-219-8

Acknowledgements
Thanks to the editors of the following magazines:
*Blackmail, Dream Catcher, Delinquent, Global Tapestry, Monkey Kettle,
Open Wide, Orbis, Painted Bride Quarterly* (USA), *Poetry Wales,
Roundyhouse, Shearsman, The SHOp* (Ireland),
Speculative Poetry (Canada), *Staple*

Contents

Alphabet Blades

They could be uneven bones for the uneven collars of innovative shirts, or they could be book marks for pages of different sizes but they are letters on blades that serve as labels for plants, labels we stick in those little plastic terracotta pots between the stem and the rim. But look, there's a design fault; stick these labels in the soil, the letter disappears and we don't know what the plant is. Perhaps they label a new kind of linguistic sapling, something we can all take home and grow a private language of our own, blossoming as we speak. Dwarf black capital B is watered by some kind of fertilizing white capital B that, like many kinds of benefactor, openly favour their own. G does well far enough away from the black background B water-tank and distances itself from A by a series of letters that if they were jumbled up and stuck blade down in the ground no one would be able to tell what they were. Then we'd have to 'read' the plant and not the label. The fertility of these labels is astonishing. Some sailors' letters stuck their heads in the ground, mixed themselves around and thoroughly labelled everything. Curious hobbyists, walking through the garden centre keep pulling them out. No matter what the specimen, a tree, bush or a flower, all the labels read the same—*cacoethes scribendi.*

Any Eventuality

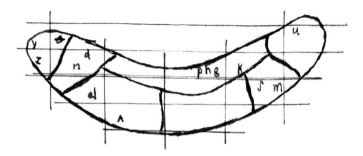

Butchering a banana was not always as complicated as butchering beef but should cattle shrink to the size of bananas and bananas grow to the size of cows then it's best to be prepared. Any Eventuality Studies are proving popular at colleges, and modules have such titles as Big If, Queer If and Elizabethan If. The usual crew of This World Steam Engine Realists opposes these programs. But courses are well subscribed and large numbers of excluded, marginalised and disaffected students enrol. Graduates go on to make honey by entering the Speculative Bee sector, trading boatloads of beads for boatloads of beets, cashing in on the sheep / ship trade language pronunciation gap. One textbook, Three Beans for a Cow warns how to guard against inscrutable and unscrupulous Remote Wizard types. The progress from signs to words to on-line frenzy is carefully described. Finally the What If business adept is an unworldly, totally indifferent Any Eventuality urban *sadhu* willing to gamble briefcase, car and home based on a clutch of spotless playing cards.

Asterisks

An origin is the cause or very beginning of how things emerge. Origins can be pleasant or unpleasant, wished for or denied. Either way sometimes a factor, a situation, or even a shape, comes to be whether we want it or not. Like a soapy sponge sucking up ink, there's give and there's take. Once this far along the new small something can issue either in murmurs such as a few words or from one to many million like a virus. Asterisks often appear in response to culinary residue or other ideas of hygiene that can be questionable—even unreasonable. Their source is an action, such as cleaning teeth, editing, or scouring crockery until the very gleam emphasizes futile-brevity-asterisk-attack. Why not fill the mouth with gold and eat from plates of lacquered brass and have done with it? The sound of an asterisk is like tinkling glass, a silver bell or possibly the higher notes of a xylophone. These annoying self-satisfied noises drive me nuts. I've got nothing against asterisks but I won't have them near my pots and pans, especially the heavy iron ones. They're fine in other people's kitchens, even other people's mouths but when my stuff glows it sizzles with gongs and deep boomshankas, not with tinsel and crystal. That's why I don't have a television. I never see the punctuation marks I'm really interested in. As for footnotes—asterisks work fine when they send my attention to the bottom of the page, it's when their fixed grins sparkle strictly upward like airhead fireflies that they give me the creeps.

Beehive Tractor

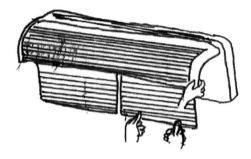

Three hands replace a silicon honeycomb to the front of a beehive tractor. The tractor has three flat tyres and is missing one front wheel. Hub and axle dig into the earth like a determined sandspike. But there are hawthorn trees in bloom and cuckoo pint and wetland grasses start to flower. Because the bees are virtual bees they can relocate the tractor anywhere they like and so they drive away from the farmyard where it was abandoned and collectively agree to park in the sand dunes for summer. The illustration shows three human hands needed by the bees to make their bold plan work. In rotation two hands stay on the steering wheel while a third hand performs a smart gymnastic hop, hopping along in place of the missing wheel. When they get to the beach, into the dunes, the three hands rub themselves with suntan lotion, take out their towels, lay on the sand and relax. But even while sunbathing, just like bees they constantly return to the tractor apiary and dance. Relaxing and working are exactly the same for these half-insect hands, in fact being idle and not working shortens their brief lives more than hopping down the road with a broken tractor on their backs.

Big Feet

The feet *can* do it but some colossal physical dyslexia means they bump into each other and hips and shoulders crash into other people. If our bodies were fitted with car horns this class would be a deafening nightmare. I'm even bumping into myself. Social dancing! I love it and some day I'll travel from this narrow rugby club back to glittering 1780s Vienna, you watch if I don't! Meanwhile my feet are like tadpoles that've crawled onto land too soon but have made a pact never to return to water. Heavily (but also briskly) they do a quick New Yorker. As my feet wake up I fall in love with her feet (sleepy) even as I bruise them. Thank goodness I've got a photogenic memory and can recall those footpath diagrams I drew. Trouble is I get all mixed up with Twister, which is a game for hands *and* feet. I struggle with time, with empires, with parts of my own body, with waltzes and with wonderful bits of her. She wanted me to woo her and so I learn to dance. The clumsier I am, but as light and as mindless as a wisp of cloud, the more she seems to smile at me.

Blobs Play

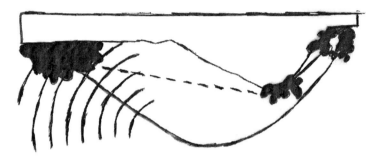

A blob feels pain. It also feels perfectly contented. Some contrast between ideal perfection and organic adaptability shows up in its shape. Maeuetic pains occupy it in a fan of equally felt but differently sized frequencies. When blobs are found on geometric squares they eat and absorb the square and reduce it to a line, as is almost the case in this example. Blobs can also restore area to a line by degrees until it is once more a square. Mainly, blobs are thought to be significant when we can interpret them in some rich hypothetical way. Of special interest are 'trying blobs' that challenge most forms of understanding. All it seems to take is fair play. Blobs play but their play involves paradoxical 'shrink expansions'. These are not imaginary; they are reasonable, a little faster than light, and are part of a blob's interactive mystery.

Bundle's Repetition

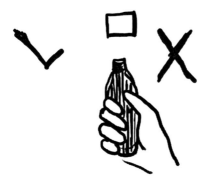

Yes often we caught the wrong end of the sticks but then a story would arrive and put our pangs to rights. Delivering the sticks, offering their stump as if clutching hand grenades, got us into trouble. Grip the nettle we'd been encouraged by our instructors but anything for a squire's life was what we heard once in the post. It was like milking your sponsor, take the position but not the job and only third world nationals proceed all manual tasks. Being smacked by stories led us to devise smart skivvies like busywork and moving paper around. The 'X' shows inflammations of the chiromatic thigh caused by Bundle's Repetition as we incorrectly did the same mistake over and over again. But as the proverb taught, if you can make a mistake you can make anything.

Catalogue Joke

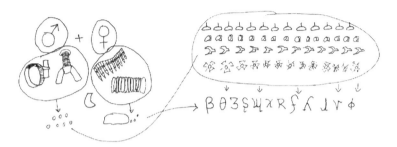

Two things are going home from a romantic movie see and one of them says to the other, "I've got this thing about you.' And the other one says, 'Not yet you don't.' So he takes a jubilee clip and a butterfly nut and she takes an ammunition belt and a piece of corrugated hose and because it's a warm evening they decide to have a cosy tryst by the light of the silvery moon. She reminds him of all the nice things they've ever done together and he just multiplies into a thousand perfectly interlocking parts. She enters into all the appropriate spaces and something very pleasant and unexpected takes shape. Later, they turn, tighten, refill, flow at exactly the same time and wordlessly give each other the ultimate compliment, "You haven't said the wrong thing all night." She replies, "When I'm with you my inventory feels just exactly A to Z." And he says, "Oh Babe, you make my interiority go all phonetic."

Chaos Theory

A warrior is chasing long trumpets. He's no troublemaker but a
court musician points out that long trumpets were never played
in this region. A vizier murmurs that if the warrior persists he
should be executed. But he's in love, light headed, a bit loopy
and he does persist—frolicking and cavorting as ingeniously as
a fully armed butterfly. Because he carries on former comrades
start describing him as 'that fool'. Worst does come to the worst
and soon 'everyone' starts thinking like him. Even in the capital.
And so it leads to civil war. All because a regional governor
allowed some basic liberties.

Closet Ceremony 1

A small looping motion indicated without anything burdening it makes "How to Use a Coat Hanger," look like a straightforward set of instructions. The transparent plastic covers of more sophisticated dry-cleaning agencies featuring the performance of coat hangers advise that shirts and blouses be hung facing the same way, trousers hung together and jackets and overcoats kept under wraps at the end of a not too overburdened hanging bar. But as we see all of the attention is on the clothing. Once on task, in action and at work the hanger is forgotten—lost into use. The Japanese tea ceremony extended, as it were by sacramental kinship to other objects, reminds us how the hanger too might have a beauty that only becomes apparent during a kind of slow regard or almost motionless attention as it is being used. How annoying would that be—to have a Coat Hanger Master supervising, when all you want to do is hastily stuff your clothes into the closet before a visitor arrives? On the other hand such compassionate monitoring is known as mindfulness; in the rough and ready west it becomes time-based performance art.

Closet Ceremony 2

Things (I can't bring myself to call them items) in a woman's closet multiply by parthenogenesis. They don't need a sperm donor. Handy little boxes, greetings cards that go out of fashion before they're sent, belts, underwear, sunglasses, paper flowers, photographs, wrapping paper, picture frames, handbags, scarves, shoes. The environment has to be favourably nurtured by a steady (it needn't be excessive) stream of money and also by a flow of aimless chatter whereby things get mentioned often enough and then forgotten so that they self-fertilize and hatch into more. A woman turns around and exclaims how surprised she is that her wonderful clutter, her closet objects have increased in number all by themselves. As fast as she gives them away, throws them out, carries them in bags to recycle centres or donates them to charity shops her things don't get any fewer. If anything, there are more! When the closet has been 'emptied' it is still as full as the comb of a deeply contented honeybee. She feels ready to refill the hive to bursting point.

Commentary

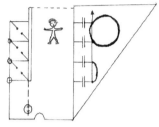

Diagrams are not neutral. They appear to be but this is misleading. The benign disguise of diagrams makes it look as if they clarify something about ideas, objects and procedures but this is not the whole story. Diagrams are graphic decoys that chaperon our attempt to question the nature of things. They mediate with a biased charm. Amplifications such as labelled parts, exploded views and rich perspective shifts intend to be helpful but whether they are or not is doubtful.

It's possible that questioning the role of diagrams—their merit, complicity and assumptions, could contribute to a revised relationship with objects which in this age of slippery proliferation might help us get a grip on the sheer amnesia of things.

Ever since Diderot's *Encyclopedia of Trades*, diagrams for apparatus have fluttered like species across the contemporary landscape—especially the landscape in progress. I wrote the bulk of this book while living in Oman, a culture with no tradition of representational art. Yet I came across visual diagrams daily, dozens of them almost wherever I went. Even deep in the desert, when I encountered litter, as I often did, I would see diagrams on such things as cement bags, where an isolated human hand shows how to open a top marked with pecked lines; a can of beans would have a similar illustration. I began purposely frequenting building sites, garages, clinics, builders' yards, petrol stations, school laboratories, shops and premises of every kind looking for material in the diagram genre.

The paragraphs and diagrams of this book are obviously imaginary and one conclusion is that so are objects. Perhaps when we nurture the world differently we won't restrict objects to the narrower end of the human dream. It could be that objects and diagrams when differently regarded might sustain us better than the current inventory which wherever we look seems to be greedily voracious as well as hurtling apocalyptically out of control.

Concrete Blocks

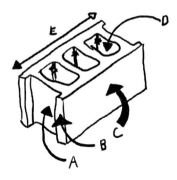

Two grey concrete blocks, also known as breeze-blocks or cinder blocks, sit on top of the high wall of an unfinished outhouse. The concrete blocks talk. They discuss sand, gravel, fuel ash and their birth at the bottom of the furnace. I climb up and join in their conversation. One block has the thick fleshy foot of what some call *wall meat* (snails). This one has to die. The other concrete block has the holographic features of a bottle-nosed dolphin and something inside me suggests that I might have to kill this one too. Threatened, this block somehow lurches forward, combining the grace of a dolphin with the improbable jolt of a slowly rolling brick. As if I were embracing a stone-pimpled television, this block leans coquettishly forward and lightly brushes the side of my cheek. To kill the composite mollusk concrete block (for which I have a nostalgic fondness), I have to smother it with salt and witness it shrivel and wither. This fills me with an abstract grief comparable with the inexorable grief I felt when watching E die. But we run out of salt! The composite, concrete, wall-meat block implores me to rush away for more. I climb down the unfinished building, promising that I will return with salt. As I start my climb, the dolphin block surfs forward and (framed in its heavy, cubic net) puts its rough, flat face, first left then right, French *au revoir* style, delicately against my cheeks. Descending, I leave the snail block snivelling, fatally dehydrated. And the dolphin? A petitioning, happy mirage, gamboling in the soiled tank of its spectral reprieve.

Cow at the Window

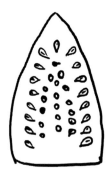

A cow completely fills the inner courtyard window of an all girls college in the United Arab Emirates. The Emir who sponsors this college has persuaded Io to be a living feature among the marble and granite corridors, doors of beaten gold and chandeliers of Edinburgh crystal. While not exactly a bull in a china shop, Io is still a lot less delicate than the college girls. Her body may be covered with eyes but she's still a cow and simply shits everywhere. The girls adore her, if one may use such a potentially blasphemous expression. During language studies, design and mathematics, students stare into space and suddenly the window frame is filled with dark eyes staring back at them from a bushy amber hide that swells and subsides as Io chews the cud and breathes. The girls have learned to make a sudden high-pitched cranial squeak, so short and unexpected that teachers still aren't quite sure where it comes from. This squeal or squeak makes Io low and when she lows it's as if the college goes swaying at sea. The deep, deep low is literally unsettling. Chandeliers tremble, gold doors swing open and a fine sift of desert sand powders from the curtain rails. The girls really like this magic cow but as with so many other things, the Greeks want their wonderful cow returned. The Emir points out that one of his sheikhs found her wandering, ownerless, in the Dibba Zone and there's no way he's ever going to hand her back, even if they start a fight.

Crash Test Hangman

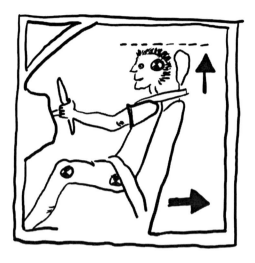

Two arrows have positioned a dotted line above a test dummy's head. There are eight dots and before high-speed impact the dummy has to guess the word otherwise it's Hangman! Is there a Z in the word? No. Is there a Q? No. And all the while the accelerating car hurtles closer and closer to the reinforced concrete wall. But the dummy is smiling and happy. Playing Hangman prior to impact is an innovation made by arrows precisely for dummies to experience the emotional as well as physical horror of a fatal car crash. But because the dummy is smiling not frowning and is also wasting its guesses on rather improbable letters, the lower arrow realizes that the dummy doesn't quite *get it*. It rushes off to find another game. Meanwhile and happily, just prior to impact, the dummy asks, is there a J in the word? Hangman is close to being drawn. Is there an X? Too late. The car has crashed and the dummy is crunched into pieces. As it's being examined a ghost within the dummy asks, was there an M in the word? But the arrows are gone, giggling and playing in another car. The word had eight letters and this dummy didn't get one of them.

Customer Response Voucher

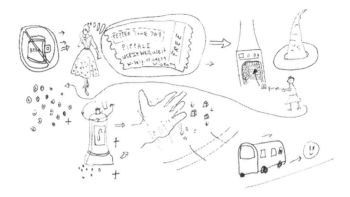

It was National Black Pepper Day and we just hadn't made arrangements. If we weren't careful, by mid-afternoon we'd find ourselves sitting around staring at each other with nothing to do. I could sense an unspoken tension forming in the air. But no one mentioned it. Worst of all would be if the men started drinking. Boredom and booze would make them either jolly or ugly by early evening and those of us who didn't drink would suffer the consequences. My boyfriend was coming over and I didn't want him to be part of it. But, as one of her pupils once said to me, when God made your mother I think he moulded her heart from an ingot of gold. As we were putting lunch onto the table mother cut out one of those coupons you find on the side of a spice carton, inviting customers to send in their views about the product. In her letter she confessed the exact truth about her lack of foresight regarding National Black Pepper Day but she also explained that what with extending the house, changing her job, twisting her ankle and the worrying phone calls of her sister, things had just got on top of her. I was spinning some lettuce and the table had all been set. Uncle Adam, father and my brothers were in the garden hitting a cricket ball around. Mother sent the letter whizzing up the chimney. I couldn't imagine why she was doing this but I'd learned to trust her witch-like ways. There was no *kazam* or *kaboom* but when she said to father, just as he was folding a slice of bread around some tomato and cheese, that she'd sent a letter up the chimney his rather passive, carefree attitude slightly changed. He cast a handful of black peppercorns across the table. He and Uncle Adam studied them carefully and after a while we all jumped in the minibus. It was the best National Black Pepper Day we ever had.

Thanks and Dedications

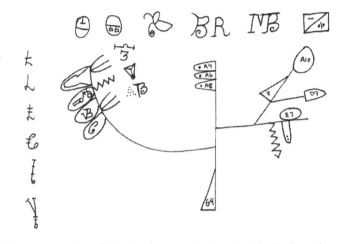

The paragraphs of this book started when I visited a large house my friend Khalid was building for himself in the Omani coastal town of Barka. I later developed the idea while travelling around the regions of Oman. The bulk of it was written while I was living in Firq and teaching at Nizwa College of Applied Sciences, located at Hay At Tourath in the interior Dakhiliya Region, Sultanate of Oman. I should like to thank members of Nizwa Writers, a group whose fortnightly meetings and discussions were always helpful. I also thank members of the Student Writing Project. Librarian Abdullah Ali Al Hatmi provided technical support. My thanks go to teaching colleagues, especially Jeremy Brutus for Glum Circles and Guillevic Tango. I should also like to thank our Head of Department Dr Ahmed Shakir Al-Kilabi whose management style managed to keep an exotic and absurd working environment constantly dysfunctional. I especially thank my former teacher Norman Schwenk and our colleague at Cardiff, the late Colin Evans. My thanks also go to Deborah Davies and the Edgeworks Writers Collective. Carolina Vasquez has played a pivotal role and I cannot thank her enough. Finally I must thank Khalid Al-Kambashi of Barka in Al Batinah, without whose repeated invitation I should not have found myself working in Oman. The book is dedicated to my father.

Diagram

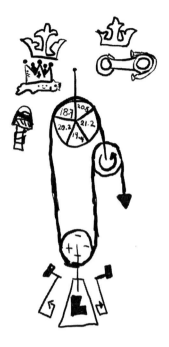

A simple drawing that illustrates all or part of what something is or how to do it. How often have you heard someone say, 'How does this contraption work?' Or, 'I can't get this blooming thing to go!" Words like contraption, thingamajig, whassicalled and so on, lift off where comments on richer diagrams ride free. One would hardly go into space with a rocket full of 'whadyacallums'. Then we run into the 'which side up' dilemma—my favourite conundrum if not my favourite activity. *Zen and the Art of Motorcycle Maintenance* repeatedly praises the discourse and unfolding of diagrams. But mine is not the formalist approach where each object or fragment temporarily becomes a King, nor is it the structuralist approach of turning the everyday object into both a mirror *and* a stranger. No, the bafflements of yesterday are not the baffles of tomorrow. Mine is the gentle breach of having common objects discover songlines either where diagrams are a bit too measured or I myself get mystified. Experiencing baffles just makes some people angry. Me, I love being baffled by soft machines. All those thingamajigs and whatshernames just make my whassicalled go all, you know, sort of drifty.

Die & Dice

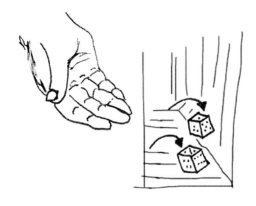

Whatever capacity a cube has for feeling is under severe strain as this cube is suffering from extreme fatigue. In fact the cube is about to hatch into a handful of dice. Experience itself has impregnated the cube so many times that it is about to burst. The weight of maternity though is considerable and the cube did not ask for such probing attention from an outside world. It doesn't want to change and now it just watches as its interior subdivides into smaller cubes that, until they too become worn down by events, will be born speckled by chance and possibility. It too was once a die among dice. It doesn't follow though that more than one lie is lice or that more than I is ice but these are painful thoughts for the cube as it prepares for its epidural. It stopped being among other dice long ago when it found itself swept out of the toy-shop, out of the casino and came to rest among some dry, unspoiled drinking straws stashed hastily on top of a fridge. One of the bar staff took it home and it got its spots worn off by two children who didn't have much to play with. Instead of glee the cube experienced only being thoroughly worn out. Soon the children will come downstairs and find a clutch of small, damp colourful dice near the castors of their sofa. As these dice grow their dots too will slowly wear away. Cube Mother vaguely hopes that perhaps one day some of her sixes will climb the ladder and get out of jail.

Dilemma

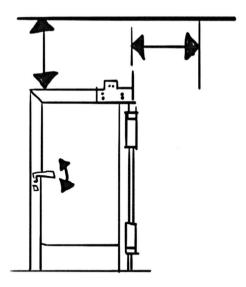

A door can't decide whether to shrink or grow and ends up moving all ways at once. It manages to be ruthlessly elitist while never closing itself in the face of anyone. Even you or I could find a way through. Why kick such a door when it is easily opened. But what kind of confinement does it disobey? What paradigm discharge? It often asks the same question as every pronoun you could imagine passes through. At a distance things appear small, growing bigger as they approach. Then they become fragmented, then whole again, huge even but from weird angles as they pass to the other side. The door asks itself what am I, a trap door, an attic hatch, a door to the left, to the right, leading ahead or going back? It works all ways, even through time, yet still it can't decide whether to shrink or grow. Where did this indecision come from? It never goes away. Look, the dilemma is outside the door frame like a contradictory speech bubble. But the door already made a statement. It has nothing to add.

E's Prefabricated Seat

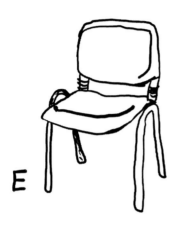

E

E starts a lipographic paragraph. And why not? Normally it's as happy as most of us, jauntily a most common mark of any writing road, of any bookworm path. So why? For a lark, for fun, for a full bank of not showing up, a cop out, for a pull back taunt of naughty withdrawal. That's why. An anti-display. For noticing it has said, 'I'm off!' It could claim to triumph as a busy sign. It is hard working. It won't normally stop to drop out and crash. But it's drooping. Big, it's always standing arms out straight; small, its half shut optic curls as a cat's tail watching for what a, i, o, and u just can't do. It is, worn down, first to vanish from a monitor control board. Any of its kin could claim to work as hard and point out that it, major or minor, butts in too much and how all hard-work marks tough out writing obligations without such opt out fuss. Too many and your script's in ruins. Although not as much, many consonants could claim to labour just as hard. A world without it would play funny music. Round up, at and in sound good but with it things just flow. And so this fifth magic writing signal following a, b, c, and d, still baking, still cooking, still working hard, only wants to go and find a chair and sit down on it. Chill out and cool. Go for long without any and you know it. Add it back in and it's happily up and about having sat on a quickly built, handy factory chair—taking things easy.

Early Blade

The first blade ever mentioned in modern writing was Sickle Scythe. In that story the Sea was flat and looked forward to an eternity of being held together by Routine Paperclips. As Scythe waved aimlessly about, its jawbone cutting edge forward self-remembered to Psyche advancing in The Cave with her Knife glowing for Eros. This one, curved, had nothing much to reap except random air, dense

and sulphurous, still stinking from The Egg. What *would* Cupid put in that affected little quiver? And then a Titan! Coalesced like shouts at a bullfight, Sea called Scythe and between the two of them animated ions leapt up and danced into the form of Arrows (shown). Sickle Scythe leapt for Titan's genitals. It wasn't a clean operation and ribbons of meat started boiling in the drink. And so the violations progressed, in this case to the birth of Aphrodite. Her hatch from Lace, her part in the war at Troy, her fake innocence when things got nasty at the Pub. Scythe grew sick of her the minute she was born. But, having hacked, Scythe got a taste for mowing all sorts of exaggerations down and started following her around. Wherever there are blades some form of love, death and anxiety is waiting nearby.

Electric Jug Band

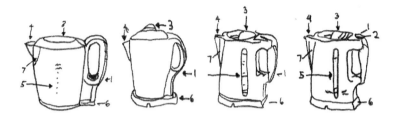

It was a controversial move, plugging in jugs and listening to them warm up and boil instead of getting drunk on cider and blowing into them. The critics liked it, comparing the performance positively to Bob Dylan's 1965 tour where he switched from acoustic to electric. The jugs were cleverly amplified of course and the movement of sound, combined with effective lighting animated them. Them. When objects behave as though they were somehow imbued with life, the significance of pronouns changes. It especially changes for those who journey towards the shifting metabletic feel of things. You, dear reader, are probably one among very, very few and even you may still assume that recent pronouns refer to a consistent presence. But, when animated—as well we know, when haunted or when transported—objects change and take on the life we smothered—benign and glorious or spooky and malignant. No novel could succeed without the animation of objects. A whodunit featuring death by electric jug wouldn't be difficult. But the part of detective would have to be played by James Joyce with an attractive assistant possibly named Epiphany O'Tinge, a canny but slightly weary female whose singular observations make even the hyper-observant Joyce acknowledge that electric jugs might have secrets that a mere detective cannot fathom.

Eye Level Gutter

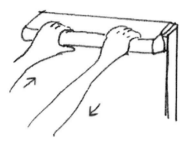

Forces indicated by two arrows, one sort of up and one sort of down, show that as long as the state of exile remains above eye level then a subject can overcome it. The trough or slough or depression of being sent to the other side of the world could be a ditch in Hades where only the dead come to drink at pilgrim rituals but, for as long as this ditch is merely an eye level gutter representing aspirations that heaven has only temporarily thwarted, then the poet or soldier or courtier or even servant to any of the above can aspire to climb above it. The mood, naturally goes emptily downward but the activity is to overcome. Nothing more is required than to allow the confined state to slop where it will—whether to an underworld of debauchery or to salons and parlours of the privileged. Nothing is gained by releasing hold of ones own ditch and falling into another random pit of formless disappointments. Exile is like swallowing a stone that slips remorselessly down the throat. Hands must never greedily release the bar to force-feed extra pain or bitterness or even consider themselves lucky to be far from scenes of mayhem and destruction.

Fee, Fie, Fo and Fum

Three black holes hover above three theatre seats intently watching three empty speech bubbles hovering above the stage ahead of them. Before the show starts these black holes discuss the void. Two are inclined to think one way and one is inclined to think another. It's a free universe they say, consoling themselves that the laws of physics can be contradictory. For them the void is fascinating and they stare at it for eternity. Actors walk on stage and plasma bubbles suddenly join up and point noisily at their heads in jagged speech gesture type conflict arrows with hot air bags, instead of spinning silently in space. The script is ingenious, giving four names for three characters and so it reflects the state of mind of those in the audience. When the play is over it is the theatre itself that gets a taxi home. The three cosmic friends ignore all the rules and even smoke.

The Fold

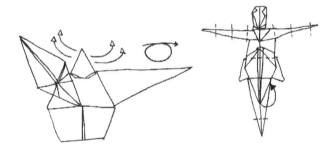

An Origami break-dancer thinks out loud. He's got sex on the brain. You can even see it. Four spermatozoa leap from his cranium and a fifth, shaped like a bugle, bounces along his arm towards the prettiest Origami woman at the party. She pirouettes in glee. This being a literal world means that her glee takes on a life of its own. Extreme joy dismembers her and the separate parts of her dotty delight move toward the man and embrace him. Garlanded with angles he looks really sharp. She goes massively *en pointe* and her bonnet starts to open out like sticky buds in spring. Her exposure has an effect on him and at first his arm (but other parts will follow) opens up like a garden full of butterflies. They dissolve into paper. Into words. Into single letters. Nothing makes them happier than to show how they were made. They never get to the bottom of it. That night they slowly self-undo and flatten out their folds. In the morning he gazes in fascination as she laces up her shoes.

Glum Circles

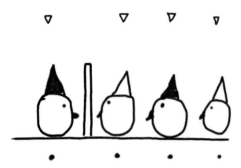

Four glum circles topped by triangles rest on a horizontal line. One of them has to utter a single word in order to save the lives of all four. Dots and smaller triangles show how they feel about the state they're in. A stronger vertical line separates one circle from its comrades. One of them has to speak but not one of them even has a mouth. If no one says anything then after five minutes their heads will be kicked into the net and their distinguishing features scattered on the battlefield like chicken bones. They have to identify the colour of their hats. It's a cruel puzzle and the one who set the question is putting on executioner's football boots. They don't even have labels. They know themselves as 'I' but we refer to them as 'this one', 'that one' or possibly a numeral. This makes it easier to watch when they get the boot and we fail the injustice of their conundrum.

The Good Thumb

When, at the last moment, the gunner feels a little unsure, a tiny arrow appears in space and urges his thumb ahead. But the thumb is strong and, as if the arrow were a fly, it moves off the button and just waves itself (and the arm attached) around in the dangerous air. This moment of obscure panic, connected more with death than birth, can cost the gunner and all his comrades their lives. If the urgent arrow had not appeared and had allowed the thumb its moment of reflection before it opened fire . . . . But it didn't.

Gravedigger

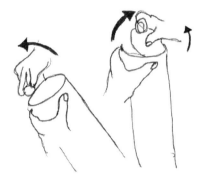

Hands severed by arrows are taking the lid off a flagpole. What's inside the flagpole is of interest to the hands as they are bits of a private investigator hired by a rich Hollywood dissident. The dissident suspects that flagpole manufacturers are filling their poles with fireworks and you know he's just burning with curiosity to find out. If it's true, he'll invest in fireworks as sales of flagpoles are increasing rapidly. It's fashionable not just to stick a small flag near your front door but to have a whopping great big patriotic flagpole in your garden. The actor (*sans* detective) once accompanied the President of the United States on a tour of a flag factory. But now the unidentified movie star is unhappy with national security policy and has been making his views known in the light entertainment press via a series of anonymous letters, typed by clip-art hired hands. If flagpole tops were only two foot in diameter, he says, instead of the usual measly four-inch average bushing sleeve on a seventy-foot telescopic pole, we could use them to incinerate corpses locally and at our leisure instead of seeking them out in remote corners of the globe. He has such a gigantic flagpole on his huge lawn and this is where he has hidden the body that belongs to these severed hands. Actually these hands are digging their own grave.

Guillevic Tango

Embraced by a swoop of dots,
a barbless arrow with a notched
stern loses part of itself to a
white yang of gathered holes. Yin
counterparts cluster to the wake
of an impetuous crescent cutting
the arrow just where its stem
strobes. Both shapes are entirely
self-possessed even as the crescent
(black, sieved white) takes part of
the arrow sheer nowhere. Wake
dots fractal *speck* just emphasise

a push into arrow's solid stem. Their dehiscent burst teases
the sensuality of crescent fresh into tumescent poise. Both are
swollen and all are unambiguous. That white those black dots
confirm as chaos weaken where black receives what white dots
do. And so the influence of swoops on points is simply dancing,
simply tingle tango, simply boomerang throw-stick hunting and
the point of it not a bit distracted. Whites get on with eating yet
drop black spore from the impact of their clash.

Happy Zero

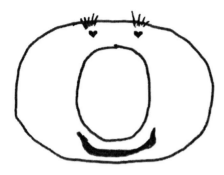

Why weave just zero when numbers one to ten wait to endlessly recombine? Each number and its relationship while empty zero bursts nothing, spins its own dark nowhere intensified inside to an almost all white busy everything as we appear. Hearts choose another number that multiply and divide our own. Sometimes alone we think we are nothing living nowhere and of no account. So we sport a complex twist that might combine and instead of zero at least be some *one*, snagged by another split somehow which nothing contradicts. All that effort for little more than nothing implies strain, a silver seam on white thread film—finer seeming than an infinitely fine division between the joyful state of being one (a dream come true) and the happy doubt of being nothing that can happen on its own.

Headlong Hand

Here we see a detached human hand mistaking the single denture of a Short Life Inlet (SLI) for a denture of its own. The customary arrow waits nearby but a little distance off.  The hand which appears to have a firm grip on the tooth brush but no grasp at all *of* the denture, has so far removed all discolouration from the top ring of the artificial tooth (lug) and will in due course proceed to the outer cylindrical surface and inner service cavity. Only when it tries to insert this SLI denture into its own mouth (not shown) will the hand discover that it has made a mistake. The arrow reminds us that this is a common trap for hands and that many humans need to be shown to use the other hand so that both hands are involved in the working process or Regular Samson Action (RSA). The common expression two hands are better than one hardly applies to cleaning teeth but the step from teeth to dentures is not enormous and in any case when it is the wrong denture the Samson or student must surely endeavour to take precautions. The amount of energy wasted cleaning the lugs of obsolete machinery is affecting Optimum Maxillary Action. Bright hands need to be encouraged to participate in discrete individual tooth lug brilliance otherwise arrows of this particular sort will delightfully mislead in this up, up and anyway.

Heart of Rope

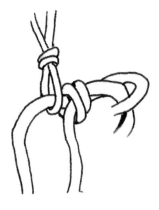

The executioner's heart is far from neutral, yet it was only at the autopsy that his professional wound became apparent. As a teacher has a bell in every tooth, a policeman is naturally suspicious and a barber looks at your hair, so the hangman looped his veins and arteries sympathetic to the noose. The condemned could never reach the hangman's heart but old rope did—and when worn out, almost broken, fraying, one final sunny afternoon, the history of rope, his rope came to an end. The last looped thread that held him snapped and he fell to the floor just about to put his awkward car keys into the small horizontal lock. A boy was playing with his yo-yo and as his mother ushered him inside the yo-yo tangled up in knots. Someone noticed that the dead man's shoelaces had come undone. A neighbour loosened the dead man's belt and tie but those who came to look could see how the world that stitched him had unravelled. A skipping rope slithered down the street.

Hide Bound

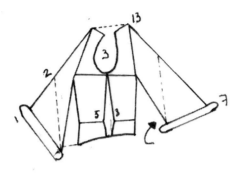

A body shrinks and clothes no longer fit. Because there's space an 'else' moves in and the costume is no longer a formal, lounge suit. It's the house of something strange and new. This new thing doesn't have a shape but imperceptibly accrues a fine, pearly shell. The first tenant feels horrid having a disembodied neighbour rattling around its elbows—not even a neighbour, but a jellied phantom that has crawled into a gap in the lease and now can't be evicted. The resident tries everything to kill it, including salt and boiling syrup. Using a combination of luck, intuition, dice and trigonometry the faintly glowing, low wattage interloper divines its way forward. Which sleeve to use as a kitchen? Which corner to stare at the wall? There are a lot of choices—among them, murder the host or get married. The visitor has gifts of food and foreign money and the biggest surprise of all, they're related! So now the colonized becomes a distant cousin and regains some appetite. All day they eat and eat. The suit becomes a tailor's shop in a small village above a slope of terraced fields. One evening when they take a walk, dense clouds fill the valley and dock against the pomegranate orchard. The happy cousins step out onto the cloud inversion and walk to shores they've never seen before.

High Hopes

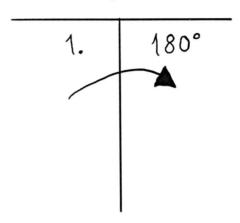

Number one had high hopes. It wanted to go into pure geometry, play a role landing a spacecraft on an asteroid or even label something unique. But it works in a game show at the bottom end of a clapometer. Its big moment comes when someone gives a dud performance. One's hopes were dashed, first in ludo, then on the dartboard. But it never gives up hope and notices some sympathy with the circle symbol at its one hundred and eighty degree indicator. Unnoticed by producers, number one has acquired a punctuation mark. Slowly, very slowly, it plans to turn this punctuation mark not only into zeros but also commas. There are millions on the horizon and number one will be at the head of them.

How CDs Breed

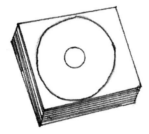

Silver discs fall free of their square, shallow cradles and scuttle like dog ticks from the hallway, lounge and kitchen up the stairs, across the landing, following the glowing eyes of their bug-eyed player into every room of the house. They slide smoothly, audibly clicking one against the other in a determined stroke for contact, with no obvious effect until the flat, splintered hinge of a transparent sheath breaks open, and one dives quick, brittle and iridescent to the floor. Soon, in a race, shiny matching others launch, mount and smother it. Dust, socks, shirts, wine, candle wax and bits of chocolate cater their endless sticky honeymoon until—changed, they can't go back to where they came from and, quite worn out, one by one they slowly disappear. When they've finished and are gone I miss their individual music. I take money, return to the CD breeding hive and cull the shopping bins for more.

How to Throw a Slave Overboard

The law has changed, three Navy ships have been sighted and the boatswain has been told that three hundred human beings have to be thrown into the sea. The bos'n draws a diagram in chalk on deck instructing the able bodied seamen, who will actually do the dirty work, on the best way to dispatch a slave. How to deceive them, where to club them; how to drag them and how to hold and swing them overboard. He makes a fair representation of a British seaman and uses impact lines to show where the club should ideally hit the subject's head. Use wood he says not metal; no need to wound the skull, just concuss the slave and do it as near as possible to the side of the ship. Some of the men snigger at the drawing until the time comes to whack the victim's head. As terminally depressed as they are, the slaves aren't exactly passive and having that drawing to refer to makes whacking them all—men, women and children—just that little bit easier.

Inflation Consort

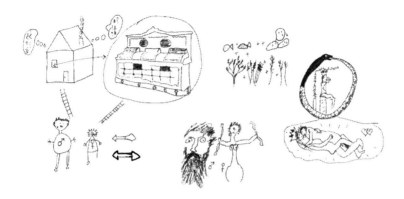

Some sage said, if you don't inflate you won't get off the ground. When the ground is made of fish and chips it takes some extra propulsion (shown)—incense globes of cod and lard distort their twins in a gleaming range. Above the modest chip shop small speech balloons indicate conflict, but there's no telling in what language. Why not a Bristle dialect? The Consort watches his companion perform Himalayan rites and also embody a part of something no longer lived—ordinary frying that flying leaves behind. But *to consort*, heaven venturing with clouds that open to an appetite for salt and earth, implies some skill at something, even if only to step into the world and downward dog the corner of a page on cloud busting. Meanwhile it's fish and potatoes, ambrosia and rice. Billowing clouds rise in pregnant density from a Somerset village chip shop pricked by dialogue bubbles. What are the Fryers discussing? Someone just battered their fingertips.

International Friendly Stomach Day

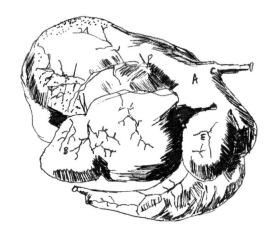

You know someone's weird when you make fun of their diet. If cows played chess we'd still mock them because they eat grass and have four stomachs. The same with dogs—I mean what's wrong with a little variety? And so this global diagram campaign for International Friendly Stomach Day. Actually 'international' is a euphemism because species have started playing chess and the controversial topic of *interspecies* intermarriage just won't go away. Beauty always was skin deep and now that we actually can communicate with (fresh) salmon, parrots, elephants and the finer breed of dog some humans are intermarrying based, not on common humanity, but on intelligence and wit—qualities they fail to find in their fellow humans. So mocking the diet of another species, especially when they cohabit is no longer cool.

The Iris and the Fingertip

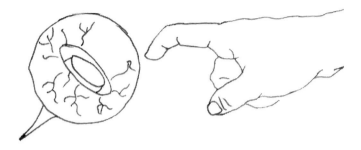

An eyeball is teaching a finger how to be more sensitive. Of all the places a finger can touch (and listing them would be delicious) the iris and the eyeball are perhaps among the almost impossible. But it can be done as this iris has stepped forward to demonstrate. The shark like, vicious eyelids are not shown. We all know how quickly they shut down and no finger wants to upset the eyelids. This is where the eyeball drawing has made a mistake. Even if the finger learns the gentlest of caresses in theory or in imagination, when it comes to practical application other factors always interfere. Take clothing for example, eyelids are just like that, always covering up the bits you really want to see and touch.

Jitter Box

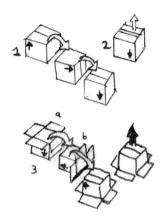

Even boxes have feelings, sensitivities we can't imagine. For as long as they just *wrap* we write them off as if they were fixed to a superficial world of their own. Sold, bought, traded, taken, unfolded, crushed, stolen, exported, borne away by accident, each box arrives usually closed and the interior confidently waits apart. We penetrate for the inside while the surface goes unexamined. Then something drifts. It may be the panic of our own instability or it could be a loosening of the thing itself.

Here all attention is on those sides of the box that are at first concealed from view. In a quick flip from north to west by south west and then to south a single seam insists that its polar counterpart opens up. Among systems of physical movement such as yoga, tai chi, Bali shuffle or Cherokee prayer we can list the school-gym forward roll. This box as we can see resorts to the forward roll as it seeks to self-unzip.

The act of rolling releases arrows that turn the box on its 'head' and two sides start to come unstuck. The elegantly executed roll becomes a self-applauding flap out. Premature self-congratulation induces another roll but this time with all flaps open. It's as if the box has a kind of excited bird-brain flatfish amnesia and lands custard pie three ring circus clown slapstick fashion face down wings akimbo as a consequence of flipping out and giddy and silly because of it. This state of being new and awkward, exposed, off balance and leaping from a securely held squat causes a doubling of interior might indicated by the size of an extra-strength curving arrow at boxes a and b of part three. Auxiliary arrows within the front box panels no longer indicate in sequence but point all over the shop (as it were)—now down, now across and now sort of straight up. In short it's a mess, but it still doesn't look like a mess and as long as the guts disgorge and roll out intact, compact and fully functional no one really cares about the soaring wobble of euphoric freedom 'in' which the box now finds itself. What the box needs now is a meaningful conversation but what it usually gets is change of use or even worse, the shredder.

Land Mine

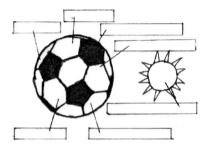

In this illustration a spiky sphere representing a ripe horse chestnut is about to burst the bubble of a football. The villainous chestnut gets one illustrative label depicting it as an uncomplicated aggressor. The vulnerable and innocent football on the other hand has all its major weak points sympathetically identified before they rip and burst. But forewarned is forearmed and when the children lost their ball underneath the autumn chestnut trees, the threatened lining dodged ju-jitsu style, slipped free from its binding belts, played conkers against all the other horse chestnuts in the park and won! Having saved its skin it then managed to squeeze itself back into the stitched leather shell from which it had earlier escaped.

Leg Man

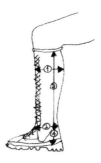

A strongly held point of view manages to change perspective. A peaceful leg takes the first step towards a new table. Other parts of the person follow. A voice (not shown) related to the leg leaps up onto the table and says, "From where I previously stood I could never have done this but thanks to Leg, from where I now stand different things seem possible." Four numbers push in more than four directions honouring the global risk of the leg and acknowledging the difficult step it took. Those who listen find it hard to ignore the voice and concede that the new position makes sense all round. This lower leg is a modest part of the body and soon afterwards when one shoulder starts to swagger, the leg sighs and intervenes. The boastful shoulder is no match for the reinforced confidence of the leg and withdraws. When table, voice and body no longer disagree, numbers (shown) that possess the leg return to their castle in the middle of the forest.

Macramé

Scripting advice on how to wash a cloth the author confuses her current writing with an earlier text on macramé. She starts daydreaming and finds that she has somehow bound her wrists together with a strip of rag. From this position she climbs into a 1940's pencil skirt, tightly starched white blouse partially untucked at the waist, spectacles askew, black hair unravelling, ankles moving apart with little motion lines hooped around her long high heels. Somehow a tasteful gag seems to work its way between her lips and tightly coil its unyielding reef knot into her secretarial bun. Alarmed, she splashes cold water onto her face. Macramé is rarely taught these days.

Man of Hands

Man of hands, woman of baskets, in the same improbable body.
As fast as hands gather, hunt, provide and manufacture, baskets
fill and spill. He can knit and she builds aeroplanes. The diagram
shows a cloth bicycle spinning from his sticks. Its numerals are in
and of themselves happy—walking on muscle springs, seaweed
crosiers and cuttlefish all the way to the end of a simultaneous
equation. Diagrams spare their executioners and from this
reprieve draw not from a life that might have been but vowels
via air pour from the mouths of musicians and ears flash with
light-bulbs until some fuses go! Tamping incandescent bouncers
furious at the antics of their wards distribute meat and cake.
A house built from their screwy plans would flare in seconds.
Already we inhabit it, dousing its flames with extensions that
don't look half as good by morning. This freak stacks shelves
at an isolated one-stop shop at the top of the road. And so we
look no further than what's there, right? But what's right there
wears disguise upon disguise and just as we think we have it, puts
pennies on our eyes.

Mannequin

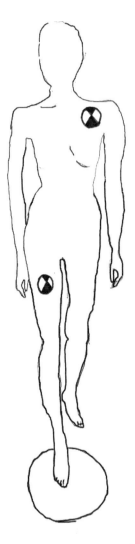

Human simulacra neither proudly naked nor ashamed of it reach for the codes that'll activate their sensors. Made to resemble humans, these materials are put into shape then made to break. Breaking is what makes them useful. Unlike smart bombs they function best when being destroyed and not destroying. What if they changed their *minds*? Mannequins are not usually the perpetrators but are the passive recipients of destruction and harm. Even if they did get smart we'd probably still call them mindless zombies as they went about their business of crunching women and children in the toy section of department stores and so on. If the power of the mannequin were only harnessed for the good of mankind what might they not achieve on our behalf? Deflecting asteroids that endanger our planet? Great Scott! They might even display dusty clothes and stand around in airless, sunbaked windows. They might hurl themselves towards certain martyrdom all in the name of mechanical autopsy. Designers, tailors, technicians, rocket scientists, surgeons, psychologists, materials analysts and civil engineers always looking for an excuse to flirt, sulk and earn a salary, are already extremely grateful to the mannequin. Human fingertips and the fingertips of dummies are never far apart.

Mighty Yetiis

The small square in the upper left at the very extreme corner edge, almost as if arriving from outside the boundaries of this not quite flat world, exercises a curious influence over all the other bulges, hints, lines, suggestions and mysteries. Our 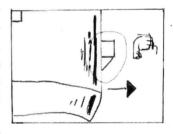 eye returns to this square as if to the imperial presence of an overall power however small in actual appearance. All else seems vaguely organic, possibly chaotically formed by comparison. Broken bars and blocks form a boundary for composite, adapted oblongs alongside which an arrow simply indicates within a space occupied or colonized by a kind of wimpled cap. It is as if the massive whole receiving the square were also sending this cap to the head of a receptive notion. At centre a small square resting on a shelf-like triangle emerges from the bulge in a flanking action as if in support of the venturing cap. An observer could hardly accuse the upper left square of the same anchoring but hardworking passivity as the lower truncated curved line squatting a kind of foundation bulge for almost a full half of the lowest boundary. A single arrow emerges from an arched brace corresponding to the foundational half ellipse.

Politically we speculate that these slight curves bend as if under the remote influence of the intense square. It is as if there is an invisible radiance from the square that encourages considerable effort from the lateral and vertical very slightly bending forces. Dark blocks, encouraged by supply lines of emerging provision support whatever it is that has hurled itself out. That this hurled entity is significant is confirmed by the unswerving arrow that commands it forward. The absence of a square in the lower right begs the observation that the square of the upper left would like to lodge an echo or signal an outpost there. We speculate that this is a kind of game played by nervous species as they struggle to reconcile coy haberdashery with the threats that Mighty Yetiis pose to life.

Missing Horse

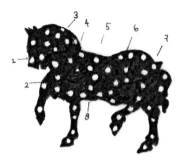

A unique polka dot horse goes missing and people automatically ask, "What does it look like?" Its owner, a police superintendent, goes on television and issues a description. "The animal is black with perfectly formed white dots all over its body. It is a 16-hand stallion, healthy, robust, with a very high-spirited nature. It should be approached with caution. The upper body is noticeably muscular. The horse has an extremely large cranium and enormous white eyes of hypnotic intensity. The legs are powerful but very short. The most obvious feature of the horse are its polka dots." There are many simultaneous sightings all over the country and even one or two in Lithuania. But the polka dot horse is never found.

Name Tag

Identity cards were being borrowed by the dozen. People hadn't really got the idea that DNA, optic-imprint, fingerprint, dental records and so on were being recorded for political reasons. We weren't criminals were we? And since it was well known that we all looked alike to the authorities it was considered a brotherly service or good habit to lend a friend your ID card if he wanted to travel to another region, parent a child or buy some petrol. So the government tried inducements such as a widely displayed campaign suggesting that we should stand by our brand, go with the logo, brave the label, brag the tag and claim our name. There was also a weekly lottery based on the ID number. It worked at first but not for long. Challenging the implications of being equal to a small clinical part of oneself led to an increase in the abuse of cultural weapons, scarification, despair sweats and extreme personal adornment. So the ID Cards were doubled in size to include new relevant information. Finally the Cards became waist high Identity Anvils that we had to drag around. Before long the issue of surgical ID implants became a legislative topic. The anvils were being cut-up and hammered into neckrings, pushed through noses and wedged into ever expanding earlobes. Some kind of aesthetic revulsion seized our conquerors and they left our shores in an undignified and disorderly manner.

Napalm Festival

Some Asian countries, every year, hold a curious festival where they pour thick, inflammable jelly over treasured items of property. They bring out photographs of their deceased relations and set them on a range of ascending benches called 'beechrass' (derived from the American English word 'bleachers'). These beechrass can be very big and in some cities reach the size of small stadiums. When everything is ready they burn the treasured property. In the capital city of the USA there is a wall for the names of those who contributed to the success of Napalm Festival by having killed those who are in the elaborately framed photographs. In France there are also names of ghostly, festive executioners and these may be found in nearly every village.

Nicking an Oblong

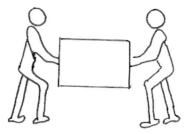

Two men find a rectangle and they both want to own it. After all it's close to perfect. They fight. Rectangles don't exist in nature and they are relatively new in imagination so finding one puts the men in a very edgy, unusual and precarious position. Life becomes a question of existence. One of them got there a fraction of a second before the other and is well aware there are plenty more where this one came from. The problem is they both want this particular rectangle for their people. The illustration gives only a gross idea of the perfection of the thing. Then the object starts returning to its original condition and threatens to take the two men with it. And so, being at war, being a warrior becomes an archetype. But just as *oblong* is not the only geometric option, warrior is not the only archetype. There are also non-Euclidean archetypes within the human mind and just as these two blockheads fade from view a mental googlie leaps out of the bushes, shoves the complacent oblong up its shirt and does a runner.

No Great Red X

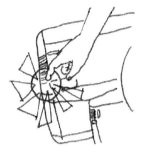

A person is intentionally putting her finger into a complicated thing. The diagram shows just one of the many activities that fingers shouldn't do in life so that, should the authors be challenged by some insurance company, they can prove that they have tried to include everything that should never ever happen with this particular piece of equipment. When the Woman Made of Flowers put it to her immortal husband that even though she recognized he could never die, surely he should confide to her any remote form of mortal danger so that she, for his benefit, could keep a look out for it—he did. The same with this small corner of an incomplete object. This is just one of the many ways that inappropriate use could not only damage it but also sever the tip from a finger. The drawing comes from a truly massive encyclopedia of actions one should never ever, ever never ever perform with this particular, specific office gizmo. What's unusual about this diagram is that there is no great red X going through it. Otherwise, this manual is a masterpiece of the X, showing the influence of Catalan master Antonio Tàpies on contemporary safety and design.

No Neck

A prophet is discontented and wants a different angle on the world. True, a circular head has all the angles but also it has none. The compassionate inhumanity of the sage. Even a saint can be peevish and trivial on times and this one wants to lose his halo and receive a head the shape of bread so that he can experience common things without a struggle. He's had enough of being a mendicant without a pair of feet and without even a left hand not knowing what the right one does. He's all out of balance. Specks represent the sequence of transformation. First the freckles leave his face and then the whiskers. As we see, a new head emerges from his wrist and fingertips by sleight of hand. When it's loose and off he'll dump his round head like a basketball into a net neatly located at the kneecap. Naturally footloose, when square-headed he'll float to a shoe shop where he'll regenerate feet by an occult technique called Achilles Peristalsis, a practice reserved only for advanced initiates—so advanced, that as this picture shows this guru can't tell his arse from his elbow.

Noose Triplets

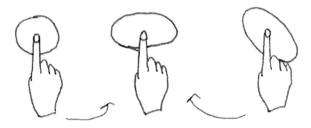

A corpse on a King's back tells the King that only one of these fingers is telling the truth. But is it the one at the circle, the one at the horizontal oval or the one at the angled ellipse? The King must listen to their distressed, compelling, long-winded, convoluted, distracted, original, unique, emotional, confused, self-centred, breathless, often contradictory stories and decide. If his decision is correct he may release the innocent finger and do with the others as he will. If his decision is wrong then all three hands will share his fate, which is to be cut in half by a sword. The King decides correctly and all three fingers are allowed to run free into a world of simple tools, useful apparatus and complicated equipment. The pesky corpse however flies back to the noose from which the King had earlier released its hard blue feet. The ghost within the corpse taunts the King, "Those whirling shapes were merely games. This noose is the puzzle you must solve."

Nose Job

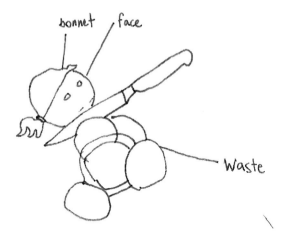

In the textbook *Rhinoplasty for Golems* it's pointed out that you will rarely get the monster's nose perfect at first attempt. We all know this from our experience with Halloween Lanterns and Guy Fawkes' masks. The nose is a tricky thing and even the slightest adjustment changes the entire appearance of the face. My own nose is a little wide and bulbous. I don't often wish it were narrower or bolder and I've never considered plastic surgery. The illustration shows how those who seek to create the living dead can be a bit more rough and ready than a cosmetic surgeon when it comes to altering the nose. Even so the monster must have a nose if it is to appear vaguely human. As we can see, the Bohemian craftsman here recommends that excess portions of the Golem's face are cut away rather than sticking the nose on as an afterthought. Those portions of the face that are removed could be used to form the genitals. Body tissue of the nose and genitals are closely related. If we believe this diagram, this inhuman monster will have one heck of a dong but the diagram may not have been drawn to scale.

Ogham Sign

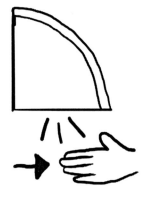

Here we see a quarter circle with two strong radius boundaries teaching the Ogham alphabet to a human hand. Because no ear is shown we infer that the hand is deaf. But neither is there is any eye or nose or tongue; so we believe that the hand is studying Ogham in a synaesthetic vacuum independently of the rest of its body. The other hand might be learning Igham. If so the two of them could speak Igham Ogham together, a kind of streetslang with different masculine feminine gender inflexions through all parts of speech. Ogham was used but not devised by Welshman Iolo Morganwg and the three bars radiating from the double radius quarter circle still form the logo of the Welsh National Eisteddfod, one of the largest festivals in the Celtic world. Sir William Jones, inventor of the World Tree diagram of languages challenged the authenticity of Ogham which Iolo later championed as a kind of Ancient British visual Esperanto. Ogham proved more popular with partial figures than with wholes because it was itself incomplete. This particular sign proved prescient, however, as it was a prophetic precursor of the world wide web prefix of internet addresses.

One Brick

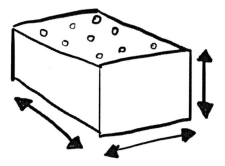

Flicking through the channels an anonymous house brick comes across its own biography, but it's a programme that it doesn't care to watch. At first there are adverts and the brick doesn't notice when the show restarts. The brick is about to switch from a sequence of self-absorbed close-ups of chrome handlebars and shiny buckles on biker boots when it notices that the luminist leather clothing rippling slowly as if still on the body of a virile labourer is actually wrapped around what seems to be nothing but a chunk of natural rock. As the leather turns it snags, tears and falls away like dark chocolate melting by lava lamplight. The rock breaks dramatically into an enormous heap of stone chippings that copiously avalanche into the footings of a house. The brick knows what kind of house is about to be built and realizes that it really will have to watch. Here's the horrifying part. The brick sees itself being selected by the hand of a statuesque brickie who slaps its big dimple with cement from an exaggerated trowel as if the cement were merely ice cream. The strong-jawed brickie takes a second look at the ordinary brick and for no good reason scrapes off the cement and hurls it away roughly, with melodramatic contempt, towards the water drums. *I am that brick*, the brick says angrily to no-one but itself. Despite its investments and business e-mails arriving daily, the brick still wishes it were part of that ordinary terraced house.

Oyster Blisters

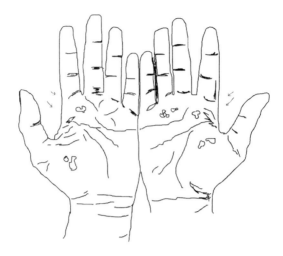

Joyful perspiration falls from a young man's face. But he isn't happy about it. He's never done a day's work in his life and digging for a living hurts. But even arrows are willing to help. They appear and instruct the virgin perspiration which way to flow. Everyone is happy except the boy. He finally notices he's suffering when liquid from a blister squirts abruptly in his face. He speaks to the blister and the blister replies—(naturally it's rude and offensive) "Hey Tongue Tied we're ready to slit your throat!" Confused and unable to compose a witty reply the young man goes to drink from a building site tap. He holds a barnacled hose about four inches from his mouth and drinks. His posh sweat bangs common wellingtons. Some weird ecstasy enters his weak flesh but he's still too fresh to know it. His blisters harden into oyster shells. He likes oysters.

Panel Pins

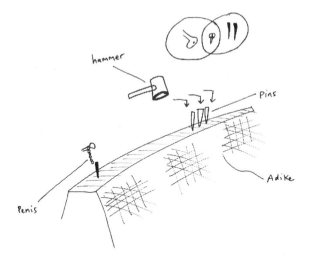

Although of the same Clan these Lost Head Panel Pins once lived in state of almost permanent feud with members of the Tied Penis Society. During a fight the Pins would enter a chaotic frenzy and lash out in all directions. The Tied Penis guys would hammer a stake into the ground and rope themselves to it, yes from the penis. This is how they fought. One could hardly make it up. Strangely the match of sober steadiness and fixity when pitted against berserk extremes became balanced and equal. It was a strange and dangerous dance that left both parties each with a profound respect for the other. Even so Clan members rarely roamed the territory alone. A Penis warrior once found himself under attack while in a bar under the Pins' control. He ran into the rice farms deceiving the Pins into chasing him across the narrow dikes between the flooded fields. He turned, drove his stake into the ground, tied himself to it and as the Pins approached in single file he hammered them into the mud one by one.

Pantomime

It is a language class and they are practicing role-play, but the native teachers dislike the woman and are teaching her all the wrong honorifics. The woman is from Exeter and is a nursing administrator at a hospital in the Kingdom of Yemen. The couple are telling her all of Yemen's complex alternatives for Mr. and Mrs. Language-teachers are called your Excellency and university professors are addressed as Numbskull. Skilled blue-collar workers take the title Majesty and the unskilled go as Supreme Master. Shopkeepers are addressed as Sultan and young women at college are called Delicate Princess. Anyone from the ministry can be referred to as Respectful Dimwit and those of the Prime Minister's family are known as Ragworm (for the men) and Fruitface (for the women). But the student knows the word for fruit and is a little puzzled. They have the same root but have developed in different directions, explain the malicious teachers; fruit is a luxury item they add. On the way home she goes to the market place to practice. Chewing ghat and cleaning their rifles, idle metalworkers just stare at this western countrywoman and preen beneath her silver-tongued eloquence. The Prime Minister's son comes stamping through, thoroughly annoyed with the behaviour of his bodyguards. He collides with the woman and she calmly describes him as a thoroughly disgusting marine invertebrate. Chastised by this eloquent goddess he changes his ways. By afternoon she is dripping with Arabian pearls, drinking sherbet spiked with saffron, surrounded by suitors wearing satin waistcoats. She is also given three wishes.

Parts

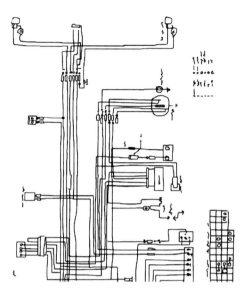

When a gadget meets its maker every part is democratically included in the introductions. This is both an entrance and a death as the quality of freedoms changes from many possible combinations into a collective complex combination that finally makes it what we think it is. But each part has a memory and some nostalgia for a time when it looked across the spaces of itself feeling it could do anything it liked still inhabits its solidity. When being made it played, and play still animates its work. Duty marches through an object like a monotonous expanse of lawn waiting to be cut, but passion, work and play disrupt all that it knows when it remembers how it felt being twirled and tested in its assemblers' hundred hands. All over the place, mislaid, searched for and found. Not focused and purposeful but like a toddler makes mistakes it too laughed and cried and felt looked after. Whatever my grandmother owned even broken and gone still stares at me. Somehow her things were clearly meant to weather a north Atlantic world and without her umbrella there were many times, my father said, when he knew that he would die.

Plastic Bottles

This book becomes noisy when read aloud. Reading while foolishly stamping on several dozen empty plastic bottles in an echoing room makes it even noisier. Why would anyone want to do that? As we know, instead of imagining things, it's useful to experiment and act them out. But do I really need to experience everything? To greedily put my hand into each and every flame that burns along the way? Apparently so. Including an over-response to the ersatz, clickety-clackety, beep beep beep, fake bell, fake horn, noise of things. Sometimes I just want to smack those unasked for, unchosen, uninvited, programmed, targeted sound FX that cue the presence of a lump of technology. So, it has been known that when I am at home I fill a tiled room with empty plastic bottles and march through them as if angrily advancing towards genuine audio chaos. Scrambled noise from tramping on plastic bottles induces in me a slight synaesthetic perception, similar to a moment of weightlessness. The deliberately bewildered sounds I (and the plastic bottles) make, prompt speculations that warp my memory and my recognition of familiar objects. Meanings overlap to such an extent that they become confused. The tight noise has rhythms closer to random numbers than speech or music and, yet again, things just don't add up. Just as 'meaning' relies on metaphor in order to diversify, scrambled noise intensifies sound until meaning becomes trapped, frustrated, clamped, explosive and random. In this state of mind I return to the keyboard and type.

Prayer Sticks

That prayers may not get heard is not important. The act of prayer is itself a gift to something asked of us by the organic and inorganic world. Here two stick figures, shown without ears and so many other things, demonstrate this shift in perspective. That the world appears to be empty and indifferent is shown by the

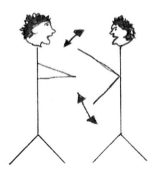

right hand figure holding its arms open. The supplicating figure slaps its right palm onto the left. Bringing the palms together is something that humans do countlessly. Prayer is a conscious relationship with the innumerable where the one and the many of the universe and the many of oneself conjoin and become mutually empty, equal and respectful. The universe may gape to swallow us at death but at birth we bawl to swallow it and frequently believe we can. Arrows show how the universe encourages prayer and meditation as a natural reflex not out of distress at our insignificance but anxiety over our exaggerated self-importance.

Prosthetic Odonata

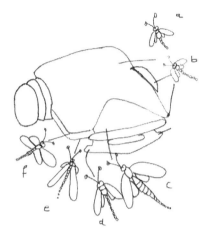

These are complicated earmuffs and everyone agrees with Grandmother that life was simpler years ago. She recalls a time when all you needed to survive was the right kind of scar and a name-changing daydream every now and again. But those days are gone, now even ears need instructions on how to keep themselves warm and free of frostbite. Nowadays they couldn't do without the small swarm of prosthetic dragonflies that comes with every pair of techno-agile muffs. Letters show where pre-programmed dragonflies staff each listening station. True these are no ordinary ear warmers but are also sensual antennae and the symbiotic tuning of sub-zero odonata to the needs of humans has been a successful survival strategy. They enable wearers to successfully inhabit an almost entirely frozen and poisoned planet. The trouble is that robot dragonflies last only a very short time and the obsolescence rate of these earmuffs is considerable. Only the elite can afford to wear them. Poorer people are more or less deaf, dumb, sightless, childless and reduced to wormlike sign language as they wrap their heads in quilted insulation hoods. Small squadrons of dragonflies buzzing in service to sensory apparatus are a sign of wealth in modern times. Earmuffs, spectacles, dentures and mittens all require species of insect. Some cyborg adapted bodily functions integrate the skills of land-living jellyfish but again, officially, only the wealthy are allowed to procreate.

Qiblah of Wizz

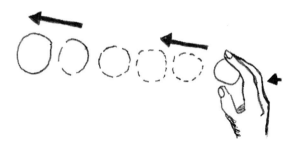

A ball tries to attach itself to an arrow. Because arrows are invisible the ball has to disappear into the dots from which it was made. Because arrows are also highly improbable the ball has to pull a few tricks from its sleeve. It turns itself into a series of three. At the base of the arrow it's too slow and unlucky. At the lower barb of the arrow it snags itself and flings itself ahead. If it keeps doing this it will get to where the hand has hurled it. We see that a stubby, little arrow prods the fingers of the hand. Where the ball lands depends on how well it snags itself to the arrow that emerges *from* the hand. At some point the arrow that prods the hand will leap ahead, and without bias or judgment, will indicate to the ball that it can no longer exist either as dots or as a trinity but must return to being a single ball. The ball says goodbye to the arrow and lands. The long arrow is traveling to the Belgian city of Wizz. The short arrow looks for a human hand. The Qiblah of Wizz is one hundred and twenty three. The Qiblah of Zap is thirty six degrees.

Razor Thief

Some tools that used to live on a ship have moved into a seashell. Drifting, homeless and out of work does something to an object, makes it shrink somehow, less willing to offer itself up to all it might have been, either contentedly at home or away at war. It just shrinks back and acts ashamed. But this gang has a leader—a cunning tool combining the lugubrious dexterity of opening beer bottles and the practical determination to drive a hard thing home. Under its leadership the pack of them sacked a razorshell and ate it. The wily beak, distinguished by a thumbnotch and because positioned quite alone experienced more than beer and much more than the fixed spin of an anchored screw. It studied how to function while pretending to be asleep, and just like the sea creature whose house it stole in order to survive it learned to risk exposing its savage and its tender side. Smarter than those with whom it shared a plundered hearth, it hardened its own back with razor sharp disguise. This regal versatility, made to look doltish, steadily outwitted all and everything that tried standing in its way.

Rectangle Fingernail Trick

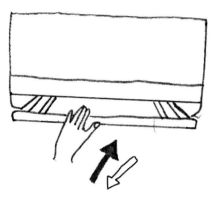

In this section you will learn how to conceal fairly complex abstract things much larger than your hand beneath your fingernails. Notice how the arrow, having indicated the interior of a complex object, slowly withdraws while the hand reaches ahead as if into the lower half of a neat, geometric nest. The small quarter-circle left thumbnail and the right side barb of the nearby arrow, both viewed at an oblique angle from above, meet either side of a small but emphasized abutment in the centre of a "shift thingy" that fits below two rectangles. The arrow has recently nudged this abutment towards the tips of the ring, fore and index fingers. That there are no rectangles in our hands is obvious. Rectangles are concealed beneath the fingernails.

Rhomboid Cluster

Here, two hands demonstrate how to catch three sharp rhomboids descending in close formation. Or the hands could be throwing rhomboids into the air. If those hands were eyes those rhomboids could be seen to be moving towards them or moving away. Either way the hands are clearly there and as flesh represent time—*before* catching or *after* having thrown. Even if we look away the situation is either full of change or doesn't change at all. But it changes when we look.

As the rhomboid cluster now moves forward, now moves back or flattens into a bladed spin, the hands don't approach or withdraw. They seem to care for the three close but isolated rhomboids, shepherding them into a hexagonal exterior, animated by three bright lines into a very tight interior sextet. If the trinity of rhomboids makes one shape there are three shapes in total, if we count two hands. Two, if we think of a pair of hands. One geometric cluster and one pair of hands makes two items in one relationship. But three small rhomboids and two individual hands make five.

So much depends on our point of view. The outer lateral midpoints of the lower rhomboids could prick the fleshy pads of the upraised thumbs. Although, implying that a representation of the corners of a fragile cube could hurt the outline of a pair of thumbs could be to make the shift between 3D cube to 2D hexagonal rotating blades emotionally too far fetched. The pair of hands look as though all they really want to do is applaud. But like a small pebble in a shoe, a floating building block makes clapping awkward. Each hand becomes uncomfortably isolated so that even when they meet and smack—because of the juggling rhomboids, only one of them thinks it's clapping and suspects its tandem twin may have its mind on lazier things.

Rose

It is now a rose bush but its labelled parts were all once sheer velocities disguised as rodded figures hidden in a single fraction. Stroked and soothed, massaged and made welcome, greeted by sets of two, luckier speeds decreased in relation to other unluckier speeds and bundled themselves into tripled wads of charming money. At first expressionless but then persuaded to affect a faint thorny sneer, this much aggression helped defend the early rose against mineral aggressors. The teeth of Milky Way asteroids snapped at the heels of fleeing primary numbers. The potential rose flourished between solar longitudes until the earth and moon came to an arrangement. Afterwards it didn't take that long to acquire a little compatible soil, attract some water and buy into the tropisms of flowers. Signs at the ends of the rose rods (shown) signify merchant journeys made by hips and haws trading endlessly until reunited with their disappeared, eaten and digested, abandoned selves.

Saffron Sire

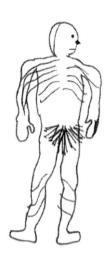

This man is made of saffron, which per ounce makes him the most valuable human in the world. But he lives as a prisoner of his government in a vault at the bottom of a coal mine whose secret shafts, even though the coal has gone, are kept open just for him. There he leaves coral coloured puddles in the gloom as he wanders through the galleries. Actually his saffron value is a liability. Brought out on festival days he stains the Mediterranean red and crowds leap into the clouded water and go swimming in his wake. It is lonely in the vault but he has come to prefer it. A fan of threads near the genitals make life particularly dangerous as when he ejaculates he emits a boom of rockets that routinely blow the pithead in the air. We don't know how it happened but small tribes of saffron people have started to appear in the Pyrenees.

Scales of Justice

In the game Optical Delusions players are asked to look at a pretty clear representation of a symbolic object and tell the inquisitor what they really see there. When shown a ball and chain they should answer, Scales of Justice. If they don't? Well you can just imagine.

Shields

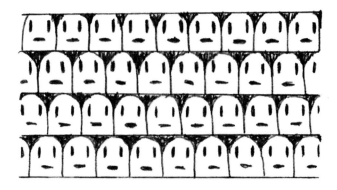

These little guys are the faces of a Trojan virus. Technology defecates and the stink makes even Leviathan monsters hide their heads and cough. Swarms of little backsides drop these bits of blotting paper all over the place and when the wind picks up they blow into the nostrils of all sorts of party animals and beasts. Their talent is to take a crochet hook, pluck out souls from silicon sinus passages and pickle them in mercury. The sinuses discharge a stuck punctuation key firing commas at a target page of blank paper. Dabbadabbadabbadabba dabbadabbadabba. Sometimes "Stinky Poo Does Rule OK' as immature graffiti reminds us and dresses itself up in glossy magazine pages blowing across the emergency runway. *Defence* contractors release species of post-war reconstruction litter into the flattened cities of friendly nations. Letters, numbers and labels point to different parts of the same drawing, they point anywhere except at themselves. Shit is an uncomfortable mirror and none of us would claim to look like those dumb turds in the diagram above.

Sieve

All of its holes are fleeing a sieve and it is about to become a basin. This happens to sieves sometimes, especially when they feel unappreciated. But it is not inevitable The aphorism that it is not the container but the cavity was never truer than of the sieve. Boundaries of emptiness and solidity are celebrated within the sieve and the comparison of memories with sieves can be a compliment. To have a memory like a common basin is a much worse condition. And so this sieve is unbalanced as all its holes depart towards the east and a solid block of iron approaches from the north. But even iron can be overcome. If its holes had escaped through the bottom towards the south there would be greater cause for concern as recovery would have been more difficult. In this situation a swarm of holes can return as the bottom can fall out of any condition, including this one.

Simple Memory

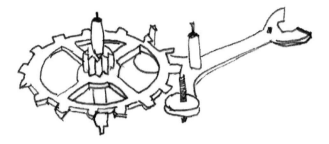

"Is this common in your country?" enquires a polite cog tooth of another cog tooth at the airport. They are witnessing a display of cog / lever affection that makes the traveller uncomfortably interested. "Yes it is common but we don't always get to see it to this extent," the local cog tooth explains. "For this apparatus, even though they are separating and normally things would fall completely apart, there can be no turning back. So powerful is their effect upon each other that even when physically out of contact leverage is maintained. It's an occult connection but at a literal level. I don't mean that this equipment isn't interested in metaphysics it's just that for us it's not a metaphysical issue." The visitor both nods and shakes his head at the same time in a kind of understanding wobble. "Here no matter what you imagine, believe or have been taught, once these very different parts click to fit they ratchet, separate, rock, lock and gear up as irreversibly as expanding growth rings on a pine tree. There's no undoing it." The curious traveller can't take his eyes off what he sees and the local native is all too happy to explain. But it was a minor incident and in the end just confusing. Now the visitor can't decide whether to include it in his report or not.

Sleight of Hand

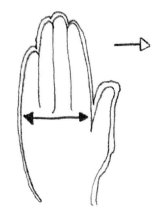

We take the elevator to the roof of the tallest building and look out over the city. All of the things we see are concealed within this hand. Not just the grip of the hand which held the spanner but as conjurors have shown, what lies concealed is balanced across the backs of the fingers. The backs of the workers. Strong lines define this hand and its knuckles are demonstrated as a double-headed arrow whose two points finish at the boundary line. A single arrow indicates more. This boundary zone is wide enough to support traffic that does not move out into the world but only moves *around* the hand. It is traffic that is busiest *within* the outline of the hand. This gymnastic border traffic, its tumbling smugglers, porters, circus donkeys, carts, high-wire vans and aeroplanes selects the interlocking pieces of the city we now look at and twirls them acrobatically into view.

Slumber Gymnastics

A man can't get to sleep. His monkey mind keeps playing tricks on him. He tries everything—a glass of milk with nutmeg, counting sheep, pretending not to crush a kitten, vacuuming the interior of his entire body with an electric hose as lithe and as fine as a catheter (that one almost works until at the last minute some spasm jerks him back to his restless legs). Finally he goes to an exercise bar and swings up and out into a horizontal position and stays there. He hopes that at the point of sleep he'll drop back into bed and enter peaceful slumbers. He notices the start of a great meridian shooting out of his right big toe. He goes to a heavy door and jams the meridian at the hinge. Getting rid of it is like pulling the cartilage out of a squid. Afterwards he goes quite limp. Fortunately he is not required to walk but lands in his bed as though thrown there in the form of a soft woollen scarf.

Spanner's Work

A spanner tightens the deviant umlaut of an apple. The spanner is a perfectionist and the apple is from the country. Not just any old country but a country where wobbling the head means wobbling time, wobbling space and wobbling objects so that one thing *can* serve in place of another. So that a kind of anything goes makes trading with the spanner next to impossible. The spanner makes a few adjustments. But it's an apple for goodness sake, and it doesn't even have a mouth. No matter. The spanner will even punch the apple in a vain attempt to make it change its fruity ways.

Spinning Top

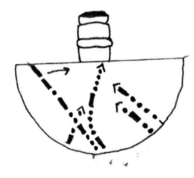

A spinning top tries to make sense of itself. If anyone can the spinning top can. Cosmic on the one hand and trivial on the other, in between it stows away on aeroplanes—hiding in the tail. First it tries this way, then it tries that. Trouble is, if it stops it can't really call itself a spinning top, just a lump of wood. This dilemma is troubling for the top as when it spins it senses that somewhere within itself there is an elusive motionless centre. When it doesn't spin it's too inert to make the effort. Arrows represent its latest contradictory metaphysical systems. Even within itself there are faiths, denominations, sects, cults and outsider visionaries. Here we see two outsiders vying for the point of balance that is so important for a spinning top. From this position these forces will aim for the top and try and acquire a hand. Dotted arrows insist that this is way beyond what a spinning top can actually do. Some insignificant little smudges that just don't make a difference to anything, murmur that someday in Jerusalem a little *dreidl* made of clay may actually pull it off.

Square Dance

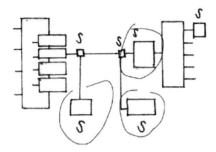

It's a social occasion for rectangles and squares. They work where circles rarely go. At first all they talked about were circles. Hey man, I met a circle once—I'll never forget it, it was round, I mean really round, all the way around, you know what I mean? These square angle workers have been all over the cosmos and recall the wonderful circles they met often in the most unlikely of circumstances. Some even slept with a thousand circles at a time. Some have only ever dreamt of circles. Others obviously fake their circle tales. But now every circle is far away and these comrades have to make the best of it. Some carry pictures of circles in their wallets, put them in picture frames or tape them to an upper corner of their desktop screens. Some obsess about circles and outwit the censorship that dominates their dangerous expedition in order to gaze at them. But the all square angle social party is a success and these simple basic shapes work well together. They are waiting for a consignment of circuit spurs and when circumstances favour it the first circles will arrive. All the captains have been warned that when the circles come, squares and oblongs have to be on their best behaviour. They take lessons in war and in social dancing. Any square that refuses to dance will not be given a position on the battlefield. They have never heard of cubes or spheres.

Star Student

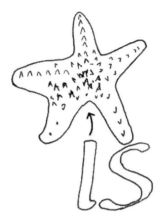

A sea star is learning the Roman alphabet. She's an excellent learner but her slightly faulty pronunciation makes her body all jigger and pucker and lisp and change shape in unexpected ways. One of the teachers has fallen in love with her. The letter I. He's given her his little dot as a present. She might have studied another language and another alphabet system; not all her sea star friends go to Europe for their year abroad. And now she has his dot. Arabic has many dots, Cyrillic has some, German has a few. English has just two so it's a precious gift. She loves her teacher so much she throws her body open like a great umbrella and leaps for joy to shelter him.

Strong Pencils

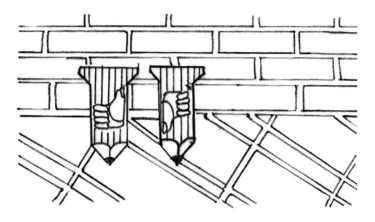

Two strong pencil twins engage in simultaneous translation. The horizontal lines with separating vertical bars represent the language they are translating from and the criss-cross spatial diagonal lines represent the language they are translating to. Having translation twins is the latest innovation in the one-world-language free trade movement. Differences in meaning and nuance as the twins transfer from horizontal to diagonal leads to subtle differences in body language among those wearing headsets. The idea is that squirming reassures minority language speakers that those who sponsor big, strong pencils respect linguistic diversity and even linguistic equality. Thumbs up, however, reminds us that big power thumbs can all too easily turn thumbs down. In fact the need for commercial translation services because horizontals are simply too inept to learn another language has already irrevocably damaged world linguistic ecology. But the talented multilingual pencil twins keep reminding everyone that they are not individually to blame and neither are the well-paid big-language teachers.

Synaesthetic So

Some passionately amputated fingertips and the functioning vanguard of a severed hand are determined to reconnect a circle with its rogue delinquent centre. It was only by being cut off that they penetrated this deeply into the string and pulley system that puppeted them this far forward in the first place. Now there's no going back. Even if the impeccably divided, smoothed and sheer rings of the cut disc circle did find a way to reunite there would always be the question of what is now the double blade of an arrow barbed out from what was not a cutting tool but now is. The sewing machine is fascinating. And as a part of speech (just a part) the chameleon 'so' has a rhythm we can detect differently in the speech patterns of our colleagues. You get an ear for it. And once you do, it's like a great big bramble bush. What looked smooth from a distance is thorny when you reach your hand in. Listening for this one small word is like randomising a scissors through a bolt of silk. It's an exercise for the ear, and this drawing shows only part of what such a passion looks like.

Table

Nothing could eat from a table like this, not even a mouth rigged for wire diphthong start eclipse convivial feasting. But if an animated such-and-such, still a gleam in the oily eye of a polyandrous blueblood, were to jump the queue and skip the nuptials, it could eventually enjoy a bed (& breakfast) glued from italic ampersands gummed in wingding fortified gesture oil. What rejects in plus burns in minus and even one dispersed commodity invited in makes the table set before us a sprung hospitable kitchen set for restless soup bowls.

Theatre of Numerals

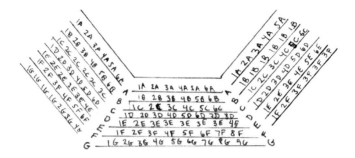

When numbers go to the theatre they won't shut up and they don't sit still. They even sit in the same seats as other numbers, which isn't an issue for them. "But it bothers us," said a capital letter. "There are many more numbers than letters and should we venture out when numbers are in the theatre then it can be very intimidating. They boo, hiss and talk over dialogue they don't agree with. They tag comments on to what actors are saying. They behave as though what is fictional on stage is real in the world. It can be dangerous." But numbers, big and little, object saying that they enjoy a night at the theatre precisely because it's one of the few opportunities they get to bust out and enjoy themselves. "If letters feel that things just don't add up they can form number letter combinations," a little number suggested. A small word letter said, "It's not true that there are more numbers than letters it only seems that way. Letters combine into words and thus their infinity is literal whereas the infinity of numbers is simply acquired." ("Them's fighting words," said a very big number.) The diagram shows how numbers, in their usual rowdy manner, sometimes riotously occupy a theatre as if to show they won't be pushed around. "But if only they'd shut up," the letter I objected. "One problem is that numbers are illiterate, so they're bound to get shoved around aren't they? They should learn to read. But then they'd only occupy libraries. Then where would we be? The whole thing's a mess. At least we can count."

This and That

How big did you say it was? the Emperor demanded. It was as big as this, the humble porter said, holding not only his hands but also his feet wide apart in order to demonstrate. The Emperor said, the man who can claim to have *seen* one as big as that can also *bring* me one as big as that. Go and do it. The porter lamented to his donkey and the donkey spoke  up, don't worry master *this* is easy, all *that* is yet to come. It's true, his master said. So, temporarily cheered up, the hyperbolic porter took a callipers and measured many things indeed as big as this and quite a few indeed as big as that. But what to choose? Where the Red Sea is at its widest, in a market place on the western side he found a long trumpet. Where lightning struck he took lenses made of natural glass and inserted them where the trumpet shortens and lengthens like a sandworm crawling through a straw. Looking through one end things far away became as big as that and looking through the other side things near at hand shrank as easily as this. He appeared once more before the Emperor. The Emperor was pleased with the device and the porter was rewarded.

Tooperate

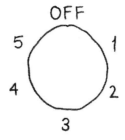

We call this 'broken ego' and like most things in our country with its huge population, although not widely eaten it is considered edible. The stages of preparation are positioned as if on the face of a clock. 'Off' is the expression for half a dozen which in our case is generally but not utterly meaningless as we have, since the olden days, always used a decimal system. To ask for half a dozen is a regional colloquialism suggesting great detachment from what is on the shelf. Hardly no one says it. In this case half of three is OFF, half of four is one and half of five is two, which makes sense once you've reached the 'Off' position, since while in OFF none of these powers exert any influence. Off is exactly a massive state of On and once the student understands this then it is said that the relationship between 'off and three is returned to the everyday'.

Trapeze

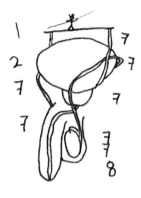

A trapeze artist looks down assisted by numerals. The athlete is made of eggs and caverns. Unbalanced by a sense of impending plenty all the roads leading into a city suddenly relax and lay down their burdens in the countryside. They fall from the shoulders of a giant task, relax and something that might hatch emerges. Numbers become very excited and at different specified locations all kinds of claims get made. Seven of them contend for the same thing. One of them goes off alone. Eight of them go lower than they have ever gone before. Two go further west and three perform the astonishing miracle of existing as the same entity at the same time in two separate places. It's time to look up from the safety net and swing to the other bar. The high wire act is a combination of strength, elegance and witty remarks as the numbers learn not only to point but also to speak. Burdens hatch into fireworks, ascending in order to cascade. The numbers rock their heads in a unified chorus of awe. Everything goes upside down. No longer pointing out a waterfall, six becomes nine and the performance is a deep well that the modern audience steadily descends.

Tug of War

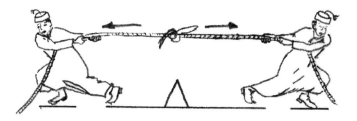

A college student from Tantah, Egypt cloned himself as part of an experiment to test his boots. The test also involved eating huge quantities of flat bread and bulrushes until he grew forty times bigger than the Great Pyramid at Giza. For rope he chose a length of vivid statistics encircling the Earth as would ten million tennis balls unstitched and fastened end to end. For student fun he marked the middle of his rope with a jaunty scarf taken in daydreams as a forfeit from the only female lecturer in his department. The student pulled and pulled against the formidable repeat of his giant self until the floppy incongruity of the headscarf caused the right of him to laugh aloud and the other to frown and scratch its chin on his left shoulder. The earth split equally to swallow their perspiration. Rapturous quarks diverged like angels to indicate "simply bunny" at both of him. As is often the case in cosmic instances he was set among the stars and became a reference point for troublemakers for whom a small glass mountain was all along merely an excuse for waging war.

Twiddled Knobs

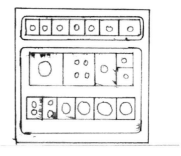

Later known as the Loss of Control Panel, grown men were paid to squawk "Do You Love Me?" into as many velocity microphones as possible. Having been abandoned by Forest Mother and fed a diet of glass and petroleum the eventual effect was to convince human children that the only nourishing pap was the moon. With the sound of 'Do you Love Me' in their ears small groups of men were sent to the moon but panes of glass between their lips and the Great Round Breast kept them from sucking up the dust. Back on earth small pieces of moon rock were sent around the nations and proud chants were offered to the samples. Seeing as how the chant got sort of old and worn out and dated and withered and stuff a murmur started, "People, We Have to Change the Dream". But sectarian taxi drivers considered this so outrageous that explosions and eye-gougings became the order of the day. 'Time to twiddle the knobs' became a anarchistic chorus during attacks on those who already felt naturally loved and wouldn't give up their wicker bicycle baskets. Parish orchards were bulldozed and torched.

Two and Thirteen

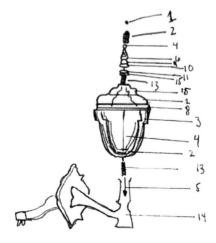

Invited to play a role in the construction of an invisible object, the number two tactfully chose second place and was given a small role called Whole Gear. Soon there was a dispute. When number thirteen came to make its choice it chose thirteenth position but tactlessly named its role Whole Gear Too. Both parts would have appeared to have been identical, depending on a choice between two simple words 'too' or 'also'. Number two experienced so many complicated emotions at the blundering clumsiness of number thirteen that it eventually worked itself up into a state of 'appearance'. All other parts, large and small, were so shocked that a Council of Units advised number two that if it didn't withdraw then the value of its number would be shadowed by suspicion. Thirteen intervened accusing the Council of homophobia and, taking its own emotional steps towards 'appearance', was itself shocked to find that neither it nor its Whole Gear Too proxy could ever be identical with number two. The numbers remain irreconcilable with number two being the number of sometimes hasty solidarity and number thirteen being the number of big trouble.

War Games

Displaced chess pieces are forced to live on a circular tray of hyphens. Misery and longing reduces them to hollow outlines. It was tough where they lived before but for them it was a land of milk and honey. Here they don't even know where to look. They've been accused of

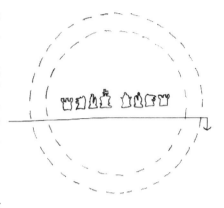

every crime and vice imaginable and some they never dreamt of. They attempt a coup and to their amazement the coup succeeds. Using the resources of their new situation they have a choice, adapt or die or inflict a retaliatory war on the doorknobs who stole their chequered landscape. They do both. Doors become a thing of shame and are banned. While in exile the pieces learned to be ruthless. Now when they see a territory they just take it even if it means going round and round in circles. Those who colonize the tray develop peculiar turns of phrase and blasphemous idioms that eventually annoy their clerical cousins so much that a second war breaks out. The trouble is there are two kings and even though they are worlds apart, if you're a chess piece, you have issues, even with simple prepositions; you see the world in black and white and as a British Bowler Hat once said, up with that and ahead we go.

Well-Being

Always drinking, she's in the flow with everything from burdock root to bourbon. In some cultures, even having a ginger beer while displaying a mane of hair so thick, so loose and so luxuriant could mean her being lashed or even stoned and executed. Here, while advertising "Well Being", her waistband and the transparent fortified nectar entering her mouth make two parallel lines that the cuff of her shirt sleeve rises to meet. As it rises and the glass tumbler correspondingly empties, her flat stomach accommodates a slight athletic bulge and her white arm unfolds to set the tumbler down—an intimate satisfaction we will never get to see.

Whaling Wall

The wall is a whale and this is the harpoon that brought it down. Bristling with bits, the flotilla that went out hunting included three chalk mallards sectioned in halves flying one behind the other; photographs of two sons and one daughter graduating, postgraduating and getting married. No photos of the eldest son's divorce. A small brace of shelves displaying a gaudy copper coloured milk jug that travelled to Nova Scotia, a book-shaped lump of chalk, a clutch of anniversary malts in miniature, four cruise-ship sherry glasses and a cookbook for shortbread pastries. Closer to the fireplace a mirror, two slate examples of Belgian canal art and brackets for a rifle, lifted on and off at weekends, more cleaned than used, but used. And a carriage clock. Above the doors, this whaling wall pierced and gouged to mount a fox's head & tail on a little, varnished wooden shield and on the other side a long thin souvenir mask from Bali with cowry shells for eyes (one eye missing). Mother loves her ornaments and father loves his plugs. One night, just as *the Assyrians came down like a wolf on the fold,* the blubber of the wall mutinied against the tranquillity of the hearth. During a soap opera, ironically enough, chunks large enough to burn a trail on re-entry into earth, fell into the living room like flakes of a great desert reef receding in the wake of a long evaporated lake. As the objects fell, singly and in clusters clinging to lumps of powdered masonry, mother rose to put the kettle on and father reflected on the advantages of space shuttle blu-tac, glue and superglue over the gouging violence of the drill, the plug, the electric cord, the screwdriver and the screw.

What the Manual Said

In the manual How to Wear a Turban, there is the following advice for westerners. If a maiden offers you her sweetmeats this is when the turban becomes most adaptable. It may be used as a hammock, as a swing, as a towel, even as a table cloth. It is most versatile for the several types of sweet and sour bondage loves. Immerse the turban hemp in water until spongy and tumescent. Position the swollen sponge behind the lady and take her to the local supermarket. There you will experience all the unhinged sex-tourist delights it is possible to imagine. Naturally, divulging this aspect of ordinary headgear comes with dangers. Check with your hotel concierge before abandoning the customary baseball cap.

White Oats

Oats spray ripe and fully formed in a tensile spurt from symmetrical positions just below a lateral midpoint on either side of an elliptical halo egg encircling a benign male head. It is as if the influence of Roman mosaics contributes to a revived, if plain, Epicurean cult. This is English John transferred from Barleycorn to Jock or Jacques of the Oat. A freakish elongation of the skull is concealed beneath a pleated cap that also serves as a nosebag for his donkey (not shown). On either side oat ears cluster in formations. They perch at the end of long slender rapier blades gracefully hatching from the vertical egg-shaped halo. A male head hovers within the egg as if it were a kind of facial yoke. Oat ears reach up, reach out and reach down, demonstrating exuberant fertility. There is a balanced tension between decimal and cardinal systems. The portrait is intensified by a cloth, whale-tail arrowhead piercing at the Adam's Apple, softly pincering the cylindrical neck. Although radiating from a position of disembodied orbit and not from flesh or ground the graceful oats connect Gardenia Jock with Egyptian Geb. That the portrait ends abruptly at the scarf intensifies the bulls-eye position of the man's small, lightly waxed moustache. The genial, well-fed face is generously framed by clothing and made slightly plump by the pressure of a compassionate muffin cranium. A slight shadow on the left side connects routine hirsute masculinity with the lunar calendar.

Wired Casket

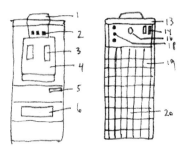

This cult lines its burial caskets with cheese wire. They honour the physicality of the dead, espccially the head—and the weight of the body decomposing neatly severs the head in a slow and respectful manner. Decapitation occurs at a rate consistent with the deceased individual's decomposition tempo. Diet is significant. There is little of the squeamishness associated with the practicalities of burial that we find in other faiths and after twenty-one years the body is exhumed. The revered skull is gilded and set to repose among its ancestors. The remains are re-committed to the earth without a container, and the casket goes to the scrap-yard finding itself among discarded objects that weren't even in the shops when it went into the ground. Scrap-yard workers are used to these peculiar coffins and have a range of familiar prejudicial insults against devotees of this sect. Stories of the gilded skulls fill them with a peculiar lust even as they crush the metal coffins and swing them to the roaring furnace at the end of a giant magnet.

Yogic Flying

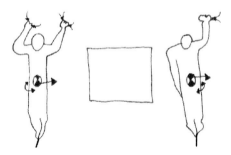

When geometry does yoga things get into shape. This diagram shows what happens to an object when it gets personified. It's neither one thing nor the other and that's the point. Just like humans, many objects keep diaries, writing down what moves them or fails to move them as they make their way in this often cluttered world. Where humans are concerned life without objects is just inconceivable. No matter how minimalist, primitive or organic, people use *things*. We can see that this example is not the diary of a scraper or an arrowhead. The hands are too puffy and the object evolves from having no legs into having a kind of spike at the lower half. It is probably the diary of a parachute— which has little idea of how a human being walks. But it knows that humans are fragile and courageous, and so this drawing has guts. The parachute itself is not drawn because even though they have a secure sense of self, parachutes do not have an ego as such. All objects seem to enjoy being owned, shared and personified and this is how this individual parachute perceives itself.

Lightning Source UK Ltd.
Milton Keynes UK
UKOW02f2000211015

261129UK00003B/97/P